## VICTORIA D BLAKEY

*Life's Greatest Walk, Your Damascus Road and Beyond*

*First edition*

*ISBN: 979-8-218-03843-4*

*This book was professionally typeset on Reedsy.
Find out more at reedsy.com*

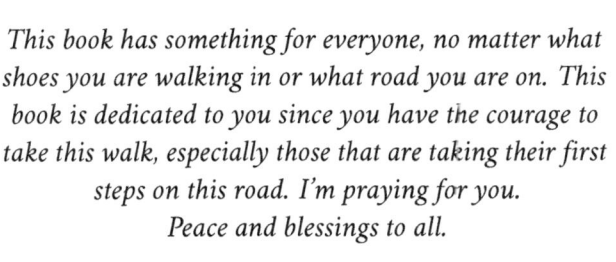

*This book has something for everyone, no matter what shoes you are walking in or what road you are on. This book is dedicated to you since you have the courage to take this walk, especially those that are taking their first steps on this road. I'm praying for you.*
*Peace and blessings to all.*

# Contents

# Foreword

**Acts 9:10-12 NKJV**, *Now there was a certain disciple at Damascus named Ananias; and to him the Lord said in a vision, "Ananias."*

*And he said, "Here I am, Lord."  So, the Lord said to him, "Arise and go to the street called Straight, and inquire at the house of Judas for one called Saul (Paul) of Tarsus, for behold, he is praying.  And in a vision he has seen a man named Ananias coming in and putting his hand on him, so that he might receive his sight."*

The sight he received was much more than his physical sight, but also the gift of insight and understanding that is led by the Holy Spirit living within.

Paul (Saul) received his call on the road to Damascus. I received mine on twenty-sixth and California. Does not matter where you hear the call, just start walking toward it.

Ever felt like you kept hearing somebody call your

name or felt a soulful nudge, but you could not identify the voice, the nudge or where it was coming from deep inside? Did you wonder, "Am I going crazy?" Or did you sense it was something from deep within? The LORD is trying to tell you something!

**1 Samuel 3: 6-10 NKJV**, *Then the Lord called yet again, "Samuel!" So, Samuel arose and went to Eli, and said, "Here I am, for you called me." He answered, "I did not call, my son; lie down again." ⁷ (Now Samuel did not yet know the Lord, nor was the word of the Lord yet revealed to him.) And the Lord called Samuel again the third time. So, he arose and went to Eli, and said, "Here I am, for you did call me." Then Eli perceived that the Lord had called the boy. Therefore Eli said to Samuel, "Go, lie down; and it shall be, if He calls you, that you must say, "Speak, Lord, for Your servant hears". So, Samuel went and lay down in his place. Now the Lord came and stood and called as at other times, "Samuel! Samuel!" And Samuel answered, "Speak, for Your servant hears."*

# Preface

Truthfully speaking I believe the "Accepting or coming to Jesus" moment in life is the greatest aha experience one can ever have. Most people and religions of the world have heard of Jesus whether they accept Him as their Lord and Savior or not. Some call Him a prophet, some compare Him to other key figures in their respective religions, while others just see Him as any other man that has walked the Earth. Once you have the Spiritual experience of accepting Him as your own personal Savior it is like, "Ah hah, I understand it, I feel it, I get it and I receive it," becomes a life changing moment.

No matter what your religious or spiritual beliefs are about Jesus, historical facts prove that He lived. Now whether if He lives in your heart and reigns in your life that is your choice. Because of GOD's love for us, HE allows us to have free will to choose evil or good. It is a choice to believe in what you

iv

have heard or feel about Him, this Jesus and for that matter GOD.

When coming to Jesus or accepting Him as your Lord and Savior we all need help, a bridge to get us from the accepting with have faith to understanding the walk we have chosen. And trust that this walk becomes a lifelong journey.

**Acts 9: 6-5 NKJV**, *"As he journeyed, he came near Damascus, and suddenly a light shone around him from heaven. Then he fell to the ground, and heard a voice saying to him, "Saul, Saul, why are you persecuting Me?" And he said, "Who are You, Lord?" Then the Lord said, "I am Jesus, whom you are persecuting, it is hard for you to kick against the goads." So, he, trembling and astonished, said, "Lord, what do You want me to do?" Then the Lord said to him, "Arise and go into the city, and you will be told what you must do."*

Even Paul, after his personal encounter with Jesus needed help in to understand the direction from walking the isle to walking more like Jesus.

Listen, believe me, this is not going to be an effortless walk at first, may not be easy in the middle, but just keep your eyes on the prize, forgiveness, love, peace, joy, and Eternal Life. This is not like asking a genie or Santa Claus for a wish, then poof there it is. This is all about something greater than you could ever imagine. Hang in there, trust what you feel inside and what you learn. Ask the HOLY SPIRIT for insight into what you are reading in the Bible, day by day, year by year. If you continue this walk in your life, you will soon see others are following you to better as you become your best self.

**\*During this book when the letters are all in caps, I'm referring to GOD, and when only the first letter is capitalized, I'm referring to Jesus.**

# Acknowledgement

For all those that have helped paved the roads in my walk.

Special thanks to Pablove Black, thank you for seeing GOD's light in me that I had dimmed with worldly pleasures and encouraging me to learn the Bible. To my deceased friend, Karen D. James for teaching me that I had a part to play in GOD's plans for my life and not to live by happenstance. For my Sunday School Class, my Sisters in Christ, "Women of the WORD", who accepted me into their hearts. And for my church homes, Salem Baptist Church of Chicago and Abiding Word Ministries of The Gambia.

Pastor Meeks I will never forget that while in Africa and enduring some very trying times I would sing the gospel hymn, "Lead Me, Guide Me", that it refreshed and strengthened me, but also was calling me to Salem. So thankful I had the chance to become a member under your teaching and administration and beyond.

## One

# *Now I Lay Me Down to Sleep*

Before I go any further let me tell you about Paul, a Jew formerly named Saul before his conversion who I mentioned in my prologue. Paul hated the mention of the Name of Jesus. He made it his mission to hunt down those who believed in Jesus, or those who followed His teaching to put them to death. I will let you read what he wrote about himself as he testifies before King Agrippa.

**Acts 26:1 MSG,** *Paul took the stand and told his story. 4, "From the time of my youth, my life has been lived among my own people in Jerusalem. 5, Practically every Jew in town who watched me grow up and if they were willing to stick their necks out, they would tell you in person knows that I lived as a strict Pharisee, the most demanding branch of our religion. It is because I* *believed it and took it seriously, committed myself heart and soul to what God promised my ancestors. 9-11, For a time I thought it was my duty to oppose this Jesus of Nazareth with all my might. Backed with the full authority of the high priests, I threw these believers (I had no idea they were God's people!) into the Jerusalem jail right and left, and whenever it came to a vote, I voted for their execution. I stormed through their meeting places, bullying them into cursing Jesus, a one-man terror obsessed with obliterating these people."* This former unbeliever went on to write thirteen, some say fourteen books of the Bible. Now on to some encouragement from me, a former non-believer.

As many African American children of the "Civil Rights" era it was a given that on Sunday mornings extending sometimes well into the afternoon or evening you were in church like it or not. Most went to church on Sundays and some on Saturdays as most so-called good Christians did and some still do. We did not go only for the religious experience, but also to receive information, assistance with various needs, to organize as a force to defeat an unjust society and to meet as a community. We went for uplifting in every area of our lives. The African American Christian Experience then was just that, an experience. You not only heard the singing and the pastor, but often you would get a chance to hear leaders from the Civil Rights era. My brother still remembers holding the door open for Dr. Martin Luther King at our church in Chicago when he was an adolescent. The church was our ears and voice.

Every Sunday my step-grandmother would cook a huge breakfast. We would eat together then set off for Sunday service with weighted down bellies that made my eyelids even heavier. We were living in Louisville, Kentucky at the time and going to, Green Street Baptist Church. We would sing hymns from hymnals, say prayers, recite the sermon's leading scripture and sing some more hymns before we could sit down to hear the pastor deliver the sermon. After getting up so early on Sunday mornings to get ready for church, eating all that food I could barely stand up straight. Next came the singing of monotone hymns and complying with other church's order of services before we could take our seats. Finally, the pastor would take his place in the pulpit and begin his sermon. His low droning voice sounded like a lullaby, like a white noise. That is what it was like to me, his speaking would put me to sleep. There was no hand clapping, shouts of Amen or women fanning members of the congregation that had were overcome by the Holy Spirit. Everyone sat quietly, women with gloved hands folded in their laps with their attention on the sermon.

Each time I nodded off to sleep and whichever

grandparent that was closer to me would nudge me to wake me up and tell me to sit up straight. One Sunday morning's sermon still sticks in my memory. I was about five or six years old. I had fallen asleep and was jolted awake by the booming voice of the pastor was saying, "the moon gonna drip away to blood and all sinners would go to hell with weeping and gnashing of teeth." As he was saying these things my grandfather was nudging me to stay awake. Out of my hazy eyes it seemed as though the pastor was looking and pointing directly at me. Had I sinned? I thought that I was going to hell because I kept falling asleep in church. The fear of what he said stuck with me for years. I still have this picture in my mind, a sad day with the moon dripping blood. He was more than likely referencing **Acts 2:20 KJV**, *"The sun shall be turned into darkness, and the moon into blood, before that great and notable day of the Lord come:"* It took a long time for me not to be afraid of seeing a "harvest moon" in the night sky because of how in my young mind it resembled that scripture.

––––––––––––––––

**Revelations 6:12 KJV**, *"I looked when He broke the sixth seal, and there was a great earthquake; and the sun became black as sackcloth made of hair, and the whole moon became like blood;"*

––––––––––––––––

I cannot say that I liked church before that day,

after that I was afraid not to go. I was taught to believe in GOD and the Christian doctrine. I said the nightly children's prayer: "Now I lay me down to sleep; I pray the LORD my soul to keep.......". After that day all I know is that I was afraid of GOD, so I made sure to say my prayers. I saw HIM as being vengeful and was afraid that I was going to Hell. Now who would want to have a relationship with a being like that!? You can have one, but to fear GOD is to revere HIM, respect and appreciate HIS goodness, grace, mercy, and love, not trembling crouched in fear of an angry being.

Seeing GOD as an angry and vengeful Being is still being preached in many churches today and it keeps many people from grasping who GOD truly is. GOD is love and is true to HIMSELF and us. Since HE is love and our creator, HE loves us and HE's true to us because we are HIS. We are HIS whether you believe it or not since HE is the CREATOR and giver of all life. Now you have the choice not to believe or follow HIM. Now those bad choices we make are on us. And the evil in the world comes through an open door that humankind allows.

But guess what!? I did not know any of that. No one knows any of that unless they heard about it, read about it, and feel or felt it. That is where we believers of HIM and HIS Son come in. Although it is a personal relationship we have with the Holy

Trinity (GOD THE FATHER, Jesus, The Son and The Holy Spirit), it is not supposed to be a secret.

———————————

**Romans 10:14 MSG,** *How can people call for help if they don't know who to trust? And how can they know who to trust if they have not heard of the One who can be trusted? And how can they hear if nobody tells them? And how is anyone going to tell them unless someone is sent to do it? That is why Scripture exclaims, A sight to take your breath away! Grand processions of people telling all the good things of God! But not everybody is ready for this, ready to see and hear and act. Isaiah asked what we all ask at one time or another: "Does anyone care, God? Is anyone listening and believing a word of it?" The point is: Before you trust, you must listen. But unless Christ's Word is preached, there is nothing to listen to.*

———————————

## Two

## The Body

In Chicago during my adolescent years church would change for me. Church became more of a joyous experience. Same purpose, to receive information, assistance with various needs, to organize as a force to defeat an unjust society and to meet as a community. Only now the monotone sounding hymns and droning voice was replaced with a pastor that excited me. We attended, "New Friendship Baptist Church," located in the Englewood neighborhood with our mother. There would be plenty of hand clapping to organs pumping, drums beating, tambourines shaking as the other musicians chiming in at this church. The choir belted out soulful spirituals that brought the congregation to the edge of consciousness. Shouts of Amen would come from the congregation, women would lose their wigs while flailing about and on occasion a man or two would start to run around the church from, "being caught up" in the Spirit. The church nurses and members of the missionary board would be busy straightening out wigs, pulling down dresses that had risen around the women's knees and fanning members that had become overwhelmed by the Holy Spirit. This was no place to sleep or else you miss the fervor from the congregation as well as the pulpit! I am quite sure there were churches in Louisville just like my Chicago church, but not so where we had attended.

What the Chicago and Louisville churches had in common besides Jesus was the common good of its people and their communities. The church was and still is a respite where we could and can gather as one, not only for a moment, but for our future growth in every way individually and collectively.

_____

**Hebrews 10: 24-25 NLT**, *²⁴ Let us think of ways to motivate one another to acts of love and good works. ²⁵ And let us not neglect our meeting together, as some people do, but encourage one another, especially now that the day of his return is drawing near.*

_____

These houses of worship brought people, families, communities together. That togetherness brought and still brings about change. We need each other. You cannot build a house with one brick or start a fire with just a stick. It requires people working and playing in unison. Sadly, too many communities have become less cohesive. Neighbors are not so neighborly these days and we also see others move from certain neighborhoods thinking the grass is greener. Well, if you are taking crabgrass with you to those green areas sorry to say you will be the person your next neighbors are moving away from as your presence turns those once greener grasses to crabgrass. We must learn and understand the importance of pruning flowers instead of growing weeds. Tending to each other as a gardener tends their garden. The more we do that the more we, our children grow into beautiful flowers and not dry weeds be plucked up and burned in the fire. **Matthew 13:27-30 NLT,** *'Sir, the field where you planted that good seed is full of weeds! Where did they come from?'* [28] *"'An enemy has done this!' the farmer exclaimed.*

*"'Should we pull out the weeds?' they asked.* [29] *"'No,' he replied, 'you'll uproot the wheat if you do.* [30] *Let both grow together until the harvest. Then I will tell the harvesters to sort out the weeds, tie them into bundles, and burn them, and to put the wheat in the barn."*

This separation in communities affects the church and in turn the separation from church affects communities. The more we separate ourselves from each other the less empathetic we are toward each other and the less we prosper as a people.

People find so many different excuses not to attend worship services. Often it is said that the other members of the church are not welcoming, others think the pastor just wants their money, or we get the group that are too tired to get up for services. Well once we realize that we are not going to church for the other members but ourselves we can cancel out one of those excuses. And how about the pastor wanting your money, that can be true of slickster that's why learning the WORD for yourself and having discernment is key. But let us remember that building that houses the church has expenses to keep you within its' walls and community work beyond those walls. And besides those other places you go to on Sundays beside church like brunch, the mall or sporting events want your money that has nothing to do with your eternity. For those that are too tired, remember GOD never slumbers or sleeps, HE's always there for and with you. Imagine if HE was too tired to give you breath, too tired to hold the moon, sun, and stars in place, too tired to keep the waters at their shores.

There are "church hoppers," they hop from church to church searching for the right feel or click, while not searching within themselves. Some may go from time to time because of work and usually other things in life. Some stop going all together. Then far too many don't go because of side way glances at a stranger or what a sister may have on, saved seats, cliques, gossiping and the like are alive and well in church and can cause, "church hurt." Church hurt can cause some that are not well rooted in their faith to turn away from church, and GOD. We are all sinners and imperfect beings and are not to stand in judgment of each other. We are to be welcoming and always remember, even if you wear the same size shoe as the next person, the fit is different. Our body language can change a person's perspective without a word being said.

**Matthew 13: 3-8 MSG**, *"What do you make of this? A farmer planted seed. As he scattered the seed, some of it fell on the road, and birds ate it. Some fell in the gravel; it sprouted quickly but didn't put down roots, so when the sun came up it withered just as quickly. Some fell in the weeds; as it came up, it was strangled by the weeds. Some fell on good earth and produced a harvest beyond his wildest dreams.*

―――――――――

**Matthew 7:5 MSG**, *"Don't pick on people, jump on their failures, criticize their faults— unless, of course, you want the same treatment. That critical spirit has a way of boomeranging. It's easy to see a smudge on your neighbor's face and be oblivious to the ugly sneer on* *your own. Do you have the nerve to say, 'Let me wash your face for you,' when your own face is distorted by contempt? It's this whole traveling road-show mentality all over again, playing a holier-than-thou part instead of just living your part. Wipe that ugly sneer off your own face, and you might be fit to offer a washcloth to your neighbor."*

————————————

These days it is so easy to separate from the church, thus each other. All this starts at home, not in school or with peers, but home. Neighborly interactions, courtesy, kindness, respect, and consideration all start from what children see the adults around them doing. Adults are teachers whether it is their chosen profession or not. And going to church and at least knowing or having an idea about GOD starts at home. Walking and talking in love start at home.

In most other religions children do not have a choice to sit at home while the adults go to pray and worship. They are instructed in their religions, cultures and customs from the birth and form strong communities.

In Christianity, Jesus the Christ is the head of the Church. Since we as Christians are to be led by the Head of the Church then we act and do as the Head does. Jesus walked in and talked love because He is Love. That means we should love as well. He did not exclude anyone from coming to Him. He did not shy away from the Samaritan woman at the well and through His encounter with her she became an evangelist, telling everyone that would listen about Him **(John 4: 4-24)**. This encounter with Jesus and the Samaritan woman was a supernatural experience. Jewish people avoided Samaritans; the same way certain religious factions avoid another these days.

This very thing is happening in communities all over the world. People hate because they are taught to hate or choose to hate. We are not to drink that poison.

From time to time someone will post a picture on a social media site of a scantily dressed woman, asking people to comment on if the woman in the post dressed appropriately to attend church. How dare we judge how she or anyone is dressed in the house of worship; Jesus would not do that. He would and does welcome her as we the Body of Christ should because as **Philippians 2:5** tells us; *"Let this mind be in you which was also in Christ Jesus"*.

Our smiles can welcome others into the Body of Christ, or the Church and our frowns and side glances can turn them away. Now this does not just apply inside buildings that we call church, but wherever we are. If you are in Christ, you are part of the church, a vast community that extends beyond walls and borders wherever you are.

## Three

### Drifting

I do not know exactly when it was that I stopped believing what I had heard about Jesus, when I stopped being a so-called believer. Do not get me wrong, I never stopped believing in GOD, but felt that I did not need to go through Jesus to have a relationship with GOD. I did not include Jesus in my prayers. It was just me and HIM.

I do not think I ever was a Jesus believer until my early twenties but went along with it because it was a part of my upbringing. I had heard the sermons, sang the songs, clapped my hands. I went to church on Sundays and the other designated days like most children and adolescents of that time, you were not given a choice not to go. It was not a personal, intimate connection with GOD, or Jesus I was having, it was just something I was supposed to do and believe.

Going through my adolescent years and beyond things began to change. The older I got life offered more choices. Choices in what and who to believe. The preachers were preaching, the Brothers from the Nation of Islam were passing out papers, selling bean pies and giving words of wisdom and Buddhists were burning incense and chanting. I investigated them all and common denominator was GOD. So. I decided since GOD was the center, I would just talk to HIM 1:1 and bypass the Jesus connection. Wow, was I wrong!

I was looking for all the love church talked about, the GOD that would make everything all right, but what I saw and felt was despair. When JFK was assassinated, I began to feel unsafe. Two years later it was Malcom X, three years after that Dr. King and a couple of months later RFK. Communities all over the states were on fire! Churches began falling apart. Hope was being lost for so many, and I was one of the many. And as time moves forward it is evident that having hope in a better world, or a better existence are not even a given thought to a vast majority. Where was GOD and this Jesus I thought.

I stopped going to church when I was fifteen.

I used to think that since GOD was in charge all I

would have to do was keep living and whatever was destined would be. Not living by choice but chance can leave you wandering and empty. I expressed this to an awesomely good friend quite a few years ago and she looked at me with amazement and bewilderment. She expressed, "yes GOD holds you in HIS hand, but you have a responsibility, a part to play in HIS plan for you." And you know what if you don't take part in that plan, it means you're just letting life happen to you and when you do that you leave the door open for the evil one. What a blessing to have had a friend that spoke GOD's truth into my life.

Do not think that you are immune from the whiles of the evil one. **Genesis 3:1 NKJV,** *Now the serpent was more cunning than any beast of the field which the LORD GOD had made.*

**1 Peter 5: 8-9, NKJ** *Be sober, be vigilant; because your adversary the devil walks about like a roaring lion, seeking whom he may devour. Resist him, steadfast in the faith.*

We blame GOD for so much because we have been told HE is in GOD and in control. With all the shootings, diseases, corruption, injustices, and disparities in the world some people want GOD on the witness stand to question HIM on why HE is allowing all these things to happen. Truth be told it is not GOD, but us. GOD's love for us is so great that

HE forces nothing on us and allows us to make our own choices in what we see, hear, do, believe in our lives. What we experience are the consequences of the choices made, not only by one but by humankind. Yes, we are suffering the consequences of horrible choices made not only by ourselves, but so many others from the beginning of time.

It is so easy to get caught up but hard to turn loose of those things that temporarily makes us feel good. Once we activate those "feel good hormones" we repeat the cycle until it becomes a part of our life's routine. Truth is we're selfish beings and want what we want. **James 1:15** NLT, *These desires give birth to sinful actions. And when sin is allowed to grow, it gives birth to death.*

Albert Einstein is credited with the saying, "The definition of insanity is doing the same thing over and over again but expecting different results." You know what I am talking about, choosing the same kind of acquaintances, going to the same places, doing the same ole, same ole hoping the next time will be OK, feel better but being disappointed with the end results.

To add insult to an injured spirit there are some preaching the WORD for their own benefit and are far from practicing what they preach. Shame on them, but please do not ever let fools be your focus on this walk.

Too frequently heartbroken, discouraged, and empty people turn to worldly pleasures to fill the void to ease the longing and emptiness to feel fulfilled. Always be mindful that being less filled leads to being lust filled. Lust is just not a sexual desire, but a strong intense craving an eagerness for whatever. This refers to things you desire so much they lead to your detriment. Drugs, sex, shopping, gambling, drinking, material gain and so on.

**Romans 1:28-32 NIV,** *Furthermore, just as they did not think it worthwhile to retain the knowledge of GOD, so GOD gave them over to a depraved mind, so that they do what ought not to be done. ²⁹ They have become filled with every kind of wickedness, evil, greed and depravity. They are full of envy, murder, strife, deceit, and malice. They are gossips, ³⁰ slanderers, GOD-haters, insolent, arrogant and boastful; they invent ways of doing evil; they disobey their parents; ³¹ they have no understanding, no fidelity, no love, no mercy. ³² Although they know GOD's righteous decree that those who do such things deserve death, they not only continue to do these very things but also approve of those who practice them.*

In this life you need something to hold to, something greater than yourself. Since we're created in GOD's image, our souls are always yearning for HIM. Many have quieted the call of their GODLY Spirit and some others hear IT but do not understand what they are hearing. That happened to me for years.

## Four

### Understanding the Need to Understand

～⚬ॐ⚬～

I had only heard the Bible through the voice of the preachers and my family members. I had not read it for myself, and when I would try, I had truly little understanding of what I was at least trying to read. All those "thees and thous" in the KJ version of the Bible distracted me. By some of it not being in chronological order made it even more of a difficult read for me and simply confused me the more I tried to understand it. And when I would find someone I felt I could ask about the Bible they would say, "you don't question GOD". I was not questioning GOD but trying to get a better understanding of HIM and what I was reading. Some of our more senior saints still think this way. We are never too old to learn.

What about Abraham? GOD said that all nations would be blessed through him. They had a discourse more than once.

**Genesis: 23-33 MSG,** *[25] Abraham confronted him, "Are you serious? Are you planning on getting rid of the good people right along with the bad? What if there are fifty decent people left in the city; will you lump the good with the bad and get rid of the lot? Wouldn't you spare the city for the sake of those fifty innocents? I cannot believe you'd do that, kill off the good and the bad alike as if there were no difference between them. Doesn't the Judge of all the Earth judge with justice?" [26] God said, "If I find fifty decent people in the city of Sodom, I'll spare the place just for them." [27-28] Abraham came back, "Do I, a mere mortal made from a handful of dirt, dare open my mouth again to my Master? What if the fifty-fall short by five—would you destroy the city because of those missing five?" He said, "I won't destroy it if there are forty-five." [29] Abraham spoke up again, "What if you only find forty?" "Neither will I destroy it if for forty." [30] He said, "Master, don't be irritated with me, but what if only thirty are found?" "No, I won't do it if I find thirty." [31] He pushed on, "I know I'm trying your patience, Master, but how about for twenty?" "I won't destroy it for twenty." [2] He wouldn't quit, "Don't get angry, Master—this is the last time. What if you only come up with ten?" "For the sake of only ten, I won't destroy the city." [33] When God finished talking with*

21

*Abraham, he left. And Abraham went home.*

Truth is, HE invites us to have a personal relationship with HIM and no relationship is complete without communication. We are to seek GOD's will for our lives and pray that the paths we choose are compatible with HIS will for each of us. Of course, we have dreams, desires, and goals, but often what we want for ourselves is not the best that GOD has for us. GOD's better is so much greater than our best.

Asking for HIM shall I go this way or that can be a life changer. Asking GOD, a question is not questioning HIM but seeking clarity. In moments of pain, despair, disappointment, or confusion we may find ourselves asking, "why this, why me"? We are seeking answers, answers only that can be revealed to us by GOD through HIS HOLY SPIRIT. **John 6:13 GNL,** *When, however, the Spirit comes, who reveals the truth about GOD, he will lead you into all the truth. He will not speak on his own authority, but he will speak of what he hears and will tell you of things to* come.

Jesus tells us, **Matt 7:7 NKJV,** *"Ask, and it will be given to you; seek, and you will find; knock, and it will be opened to you.*

A new believer or long time Christian that may be seeking a better personal relationship with GOD can be turned off by what they do not understand in the Bible or GOD's WORD being spoken to them.

22

Walking your road to Damascus cannot and should not be done alone. Paul was not alone on his journey to Damascus. After he heard the "Voice", he needed help leading him to understanding. **Acts 9: 7-8**, *"And the men who journeyed with him stood speechless, hearing a voice but seeing no one. Then Saul arose from the ground, and when his eyes were opened, he saw no one. But they led him by the hand and brought him into Damascus."*

Many people do not develop their faith because they do not understand the bridge that gets them from accepting Jesus to that larger understanding of what it means to be a part of the Body of Christ and truly being born again. I did not! It took me years to get it, to have my aha moment! When I had my personal experience with Jesus, I accepted that He was, is and has been. That was it, but that was not enough. I did not know the Bible or the importance of understanding it. Truly did not understand that it is our road map to walking our journey on this Earth. Did not know or understand it's trans-formative power! The Bible is a key that unlocks so many mysteries about GOD and us.

So, I did not know or have GOD's promises to cling to when I didn't have anything to hold on to.I did not know:

**Deuteronomy 31:8,** *"It is the Lord who goes before you. He will be with you; he will not leave you or forsake* *you. Do not fear or be dismayed."*

**Jeremiah 29:11-13**, *For I know the plans I have for you, declares the Lord, plans for welfare and not for evil, to give you a future and a hope. Then you will call upon me and come and pray to me, and I will hear you. You will seek me and find me, when you seek me with all your heart.*

**Isiah 41:10**, *Fear not, for I am with you; be not dismayed, for I am your God; I will strengthen you, I will help you, I will uphold you with my righteous right hand.*

**Romans 8:28**, *And we know that for those who love God all things work together for good, for those who are called according to his purpose.*

I did not know any of these promises or over the 3,000 others mentioned in the Bible. I did not know GOD for myself. I believed there was a GOD, but not GOD just for me. Yep, there's GOD just for you and that is something that gets missed with too many believers or want to be believers. I did not and many others don't fully understand **John 3:16** was about personal relationship.

**John 3:16 NLT,** *" For God so loved the world that he gave HIS one and only Son, that whoever believes in him shall not perish but have eternal life."*

You see that whoever is you, it is me and all those who choose to believe. GOD loves us so much that HE gave us HIS Son to be sacrificed for us once and for all.

As I began to fade away from church, I cannot recall any member coming by or calling to see why I was absent after being faithful with my attendance as in the past. Not even my mother.

I would sometimes feel shunned or like an outsider when I would pop into a church from time to time. Some of the sisters would glance at me over their shoulder with the rolling of the eyes as they leaned over and whispered something to the next sister. And we cannot overlook the brothers looking you up and down. A smile and most definitely the right kind of hug could have kept me coming back since I was searching for that church familiarity. Searching for something to fill the emptiness in my core. Longing to be embraced, seeking love but feeling unwelcome.

This is a big problem in our families, communities, and churches today, we let each other fade into the woodwork. People and especially our children are being traumatized times daily and far too much of it is coming from inside the home. In our neighborhoods, many of us are not very neighborly these days, the village is disintegrating. With generation after generation embracing technology, we are more connected to our phones than each other. In our churches when we see members MIA some do not even bother to check on or even inquire about their brother or sister in Christ. No wonder our relationships with GOD, the church and each other are fractured. We let each other fade into the woodwork, or step over them on our way. As families, neighborhoods, communities, and churches we are falling apart. We must unite to progress in all that we do as a people, as the Church. Stand, but do not stand alone. There is strength in numbers.

---

**1 Corinthians 12 NIV,** <sup>20</sup> *"But now indeed there are many members, yet one body.* <sup>21</sup> *And the eye cannot say to the hand, "I have no need of you"; nor again the head to the feet, "I have no need of you."*

<sup>26</sup> *"And if one member suffers, all the members suffer with it; or if one member is honored, all the members rejoice with it.* <sup>27</sup> *Now you are the body of Christ, and members individually."*

---

**Ephesians 4:16,** *"He makes the whole body fit together perfectly. As each part does its own special work, it helps the other parts grow, so that the whole body is healthy and growing and full of love."*

---

The African American Church Experience or any of your early church experiences are not just something you did, but it was a part of who you were. I did not fully grasp this until living in Africa in

2005. When someone asked me what I missed most about living in the states, surprisingly my answer was church. Church?! It came out of my mouth so fast it caught me off guard. I was not a frequent church goer and had not been for years I would watch sermons on TV from time to time and would visit a random church every now and then. Even though I had not been a frequent church goer it was a part of my familiar so maybe that is what I missed in a distant land. I felt if I were connected to the body of believers, it could help me feel less alone so far away from home. Church as I knew it was the binding fabric of a strong community, the extension of family.

## Five

*Finding my Way*

I listened to someone that barely knew me tell me that I should read the Bible every day. Huh, what? I did not meet him in a church or on a street corner preaching, but in a Reggae Club. Yep, swaying to the beat this brother saw my aura, sensed the light hidden. People can see the hole in your soul so be careful the mask you choose to wear until the day you no longer need one. This brother was a blessing, he recognized a beauty, a light that lived within me that I did not see in myself when I looked in the mirror. I considered him a messenger that GOD sent to point me to the road of redemption, my new birth. He did not lay hands on me, simply told me to read the Bible every day from cover to cover, verse by verse, chapter by chapter, year by year, and pray daily. GOD bless you Pablove Black!

Reading the KJV of the Bible was confusing in so many ways; some books seemed to be repetitive, so much is not in chronological order, so much violence, so much, so much so much. I did not understand so much, but I did not give up and GOD's WORD began to reveal its' mysteries to me. The more I read the more I understood and that is a continuing to this day. After a few years of reading the KJV version I switched to the NIV, then the NLT versions and reading it seemed so much easier. There are so many versions of the Bible now days, but what I noticed is that so much of the spiritual interactions are being left out of the newer versions. Like the old saying goes, "things get lost in translation". Since we are far more than flesh and blood, I believe being aware of these spiritual interactions are important to know. We need to know and be aware of the super-natural world as well as the natural. The SPIRIT that leads believers is just that, a super-natural spirit.

**Ephesians 6: 10-12 NIV**, *Finally, be strong in the Lord and in his mighty power.* *11 Put on the full armor of God, so that you can take your stand against the devil's schemes.* *12 For our struggle is not against flesh and blood, but against the rulers, against the authorities, against the powers of this dark world and against the spiritual forces of evil in the heavenly realms.*

Don't give up, keep reading your Bible, not just occasionally, but every day. It will unfold for you as it did me the more you seek to understand it. I learned that doing your best is a daily process and that process will lead to a new and better you if you apply yourself as you continue to read on day after day, year after year. This is when things really get good! Trust GOD first but trust this, it gets so much better. I am a witness!

I did not get the concept, "being born again," thing that you hear people speak of, and that is also in the Bible.

. **John:3-4 TLB**, *3 Jesus replied, "With all the earnestness I possess I tell you this: Unless you are born again, you can never get into the Kingdom of God." 4 "Born again!" exclaimed Nicodemus. "What do you mean? How can an old man go back into his mother's womb and be born again?"*

It is another "Aha" moment when you realize the things that used to interest you no longer attract you. Life feels lighter and the grass is most definitely greener. Not only others, but you will also recognize the light, the beauty that is living in you and you will know, not just believe that it is GOD's light illuminating you and your life. You begin to know and feel your worth and nothing or no one can diminish or devalue you. No matter how ugly life can be you are precious in the sight of the LORD.

You will realize you're different! There it is, a new you, born again

**Luke 12: 6-7 MSG Bible**, *"What's the price of two or three pet canaries? Some loose change, right? But God never overlooks a single one. And he pays even greater attention to you, down to the last detail—even numbering the hairs on your head! So don't be intimidated by all this bully talk. You're worth more than a million canaries."*

As you read, pray and ask GOD to give you understanding of the greatest history book ever written. Ask for understanding of its relevance then, now and specifically to you right now and each time you read it.

**John 16:13 AMP,** *But when He, the Spirit of Truth, comes, He will guide you into all the truth [full and complete truth]. For He will not speak on His own initiative, but He will speak whatever He hears [from the Father—the message regarding the Son], and He will disclose to you what is to come [in the future].*

Once the old dead skin is sloughed off do not regret your past. Uh, uh, no, the former way of life is a benefit to you now and others.

**Psalm 139:14 NKJV**, *"I will praise You, for Marvelous are Your works, I am fearfully and wonderfully made; And that my soul knows very well."*

Now you have a story to tell, a witness to another how to overcome some things in life that may have held you captive. Go ahead, show, and tell! Let them see the new you as you tell them what GOD has done for you and brought you through.

I could go on and on with more scriptures and testimonies, but this is not about me, but you.

Do not give up on GOD, your growth, your freedom, your best life. Be like a Berean in the Bible; **Acts 11:17 NASB,** *"Now these were more noble-minded than those in Thessalonica, for they received the word with great eagerness, examining the Scriptures daily to see whether these things were so."*

# Six

# Getting Back to Church

One more thing before I wind this up for now. Go to church! Not just a Bible preaching, but a Bible teaching church. Before I go any further, I will say that is easier said than done. I did not go to church for years, even after I accepted Jesus.

I had many excuses for not going to church over the years, but deep inside I had this inner yearning to be part of a church community. Some Sundays I would just be getting home from hanging out or in all night. Quite often I would be getting ready to sleep around the time most church goers were getting ready to go to church or working a twelve-hour shift on Sundays. Nor did I take the initiative to find a church in my area. I used to say, "I'm spiritual" and didn't need to go to church. Well, that was just another lie I bought into.

I found some solace in watching different churches on TV from time to time, but rarely attended a service then. It was not until while I was living in Africa and an acquaintance asked me what I missed most from the USA. It was a great question and I thought for just a brief time and replied, "Hmm, that's strange because I miss church!"! Now that is something, I thought. When I was alone later that day and through the night, I pondered my response trying to understand it and me.

While living in Africa I could get just about everything I could get while living in the states, even if I had someone mail it to me. But I could not get that church feeling, that unexplained sensation when two or three or more are gathered in the same place. **Matt 18:20 MSG**, *"When two or three of you are together because of me, you can be sure that I'll be there".*

No watching on TV or tuning to a gospel station on the radio at that time. The country I was living in was and is ninety-two percent Islamic so when I would hear their calls to prayer from the local mosque, I would yearn more for a place I could worship. I visited churches that did not give me that feeling my spirit was longing for until one Sunday I found one that suited me, filled me, taught me, spoke to me. I also found a church home once I moved back to the states.

Look for a house of worship that welcomes you, whether in person or online. Remember that church is not a building. The building houses the church, but each member has a part to play in and outside the building. Apply yourself to the new members, or Sunday school classes, and volunteer in the church you choose.

**Proverbs 27:17 MSG**, *"You use steel to sharpen steel, and one friend sharpens another."*

The more you get involved you will be inspired to participate in the sharing blessings, even receiving an overflow of blessings. Your participation may be the key to unlocking another person's heart to receive Christ. And do you know what happens when something flows over? It spills over to others and they are blessed because of you.

## Seven

# Keep on Walking

Now that you are developing your faith and understanding don't let life's obstacles trip you up because your walk is not going to always be a smooth easy road. And when you do trip, and maybe stumble, even fall be encouraged. Know that GOD always has what's best for you in store and HE warns you in advance not to lose heart because days like that will happen in this life, but HE's always with you.

**Matthew 11:28-30**, *Are you tired? Worn out? Burned out on religion? Come to me. Get away with me and you'll recover your life. I'll show you how to take a real rest. Walk with me and work with me—watch how I do it. Learn the unforced rhythms of grace. I won't lay anything heavy or ill-fitting on you. Keep company with me and you'll learn to live freely and lightly."*

**John 16: 33 ESV**, *Peace. In the world you will have tribulation. But take heart; I have overcome the world." I have said these things to you, that in me you may have*

So, when those storms come hold fast to what you're learning or have learned from the WORD. Put that faith to work. To build faith you must put it to work like a muscle. To build muscle you got to work at it, such is faith. **James 2: 17 MSG**, *Thus also faith by itself, if it does not have works, is dead.*

Don't try facing hardships alone, call on GOD and HIS resourceful army to help you. Pray, stay in the WORD, use your spiritual gifts and strength, and let others of the church help you in the way GOD has equipped them to. This can be difficult for some, especially for those that consider themselves self-reliant. You have heard the saying, "it's better to give than receive", well that's not always true. As believers, Christians, we are always receiving, mercy grace, forgiveness salvation, patience and the blessings continue. Learn how to receive strength, encouragement, a helping hand or whatever is being extended to you in love. And wait patiently for GOD to provide what it is you are in need of.

**James 5: 13-15 MSG**, *Are you hurting? Pray. Do you feel great? Sing praises. Are you sick? Call the church leaders together to pray and anoint you with oil in the name of the Master. Believing-prayer will heal you, and Jesus will put you on your feet. And if you've* *sinned, you'll be forgiven—healed inside and out.*

**Isaiah 40:31 NKJV**, *But those who wait on the Lord, shall renew their strength; They shall mount up with wings like eagles, they shall run and not be weary, they shall walk and not faint.*

Now the street, avenue, road or wherever may not be the Damascus Road, but it's where you were called. The blessing is you have been called.

HalleluJAH!

# Questions

*Notes*

# *About the Author*

Victoria D Blakey is from Chicago, IL, but spent her early childhood winters in Louisville, KY. Victoria's faith, family, and service to others are the most important facets of her life. She also enjoys traveling, cooking traditional meals with a vegetarian spin, and laughter.

She is the founder and director of, "It's Nice To Be Nice International (INTBN)", a non-profit organization that provides a free basic literacy program for women. The "Female Adult Literacy Program, FALP", is for females seventeen-years and older in Gambia, West Africa. Victoria is a retired Practical

Nurse and an advocate for women's health issues and beyond.

Victoria currently divides her time between Chicago, Il and Gambia, West Africa where she is directs the "FALP" program for INTBN. She is a member of a church on both continents, Salem Baptist Church of Chicago and Abiding Word Ministry of The Gambia.

Victoria is aka as N'della, a name given to her on her first visit to Senegal, West Africa in 1999. The name, N'della means beauty that shines from within. The name is from the Serer Tribe of West Africa.

Some of her early life experiences are detailed in her self-published online novel, "Never a Mile From Home".

Part of the proceeds of this book will go towards INTBN's functions.

**You can connect with me on:**

🌐 http://intbn.org

🔲 https://www.facebook.com/victoria.d.blakey

🖉 https://www.facebook.com/Its-Nice-To-Be-Nice-INTBN-International-142784572402620

www.ingramcontent.com/pod-product-compliance
Lightning Source LLC
Chambersburg PA
CBHW061719120626
46550CB00003B/1286

* 9 7 9 8 2 1 8 0 3 8 4 3 4 *